Little Pebble™

What Are Tornadoes?

by Mari Schuh

PEBBLE
a capstone imprint

Little Pebble is published by Pebble
1710 Roe Crest Drive,
North Mankato, Minnesota 56003
www.capstonepub.com

Library of Congress Cataloging-in-Publication Data
Names: Schuh, Mari C., 1975–author.
Title: What are tornadoes? / by Mari Schuh.
Description: North Mankato, Minnesota : Pebble, a Capstone imprint, [2019] | Series: Little pebble. Wicked weather | Audience: Ages 4–8.
Identifiers: LCCN 2018029805 (print) | LCCN 2018031693 (ebook) | ISBN 9781977103352 (eBook PDF) | ISBN 9781977103284 (hardcover) | ISBN 9781977105455 (paperback)
Subjects: LCSH: Tornadoes—Juvenile literature.
Classification: LCC QC955.2 (ebook) | LCC QC955.2 .S393 2019 (print) | DDC 551.55/3—dc23
LC record available at https://lccn.loc.gov/2018029805

Editorial Credits
Nikki Potts, editor; Kyle Grenz, designer;
Heather Mauldin, media researcher; Tori Abraham, production specialist

Photo Credits
Getty Images: Barcroft Media, 7, Charriau Pierre, 19; iStockphoto: clintspencer, 11, 13, eyecrave, 21, SBSArtDept, 17; Shutterstock: Amanda Carden, cover, Cammie Czuchnicki, 9, Malte Pott, 15, Minerva Studio, 5

Printed in the United States 6797

Table of Contents

What Is a Tornado?

The sky is dark.

A tube of air spins down from a cloud.

It hits the ground.

It is a tornado!

A tornado has strong winds.

It is also called a twister.

It starts in a storm cloud.

Warm air goes up.

It meets cold, dry air.

A tornado spins.

It moves across the land.

See it go!

Buildings are torn apart.
Trees are ripped
out of the ground.

A tornado can be quick. Most last less than 10 minutes.

Staying Safe

A loud siren goes off.

It is a warning.

Go inside.

Stay away from windows.

Go now!

The storm ends.

People clean up.

They are OK!

Glossary

siren—a device that makes a loud sound; sirens are often used as signals or warnings

torn—pulled apart by a strong force

tornado—a powerful rotating column of air that goes from a thunderstorm to the ground

warning—something that makes people aware of danger

Read More

Rivera, Andrea. *Tornadoes.* Zoom In On Natural Disasters. Minneapolis: Abdo Zoom, 2018.

Schuetz, Kristin. *Severe Weather.* Understanding Weather. Minneapolis: Bellwether Media, 2016.

Shores, Lori. *How to Build a Tornado in a Bottle.* Hands-On Science Fun. North Mankato, Minn.: Capstone Press, 2018.

Internet Sites

Use FactHound to find Internet sites related to this book.

Visit www.facthound.com

Just type in 9781977103284 and go.

Critical Thinking Questions

1. What is another name for a tornado?
2. Name one way people can stay safe during a tornado.
3. How might people know a tornado is coming?

Index